The True Book
of Animal Homes

Allison Titus

Distributed by University Press of New England
Hanover and London

No part of this book may be used or reproduced in any manner without written permission except in the case of brief quotations embodied in critical articles and reviews. Please direct inquiries to:

Saturnalia Books
105 Woodside Rd.
Ardmore, PA 19003
info@saturnaliabooks.com

ISBN: 978-0-9980534-2-4
Library of Congress Control Number: 2016952337

Book Design by Saturnalia Books
Printing by McNaughton & Gunn
Cover Design:

Distributed by:
University Press of New England
1 Court Street
Lebanon, NH 03766
800-421-1561

Poems from this book were originally published in the following journals:

Black Warrior Review; Blackbird; Catch Up; A Public Space; Barrow Street; RealPoetik; Unsaid; Gulf Coast; Boston Review; Tin House; Gigantic Sequins; Pinwheel; La Vague Journal; MiPOesias.

.

For the mongrels

I must be a little rabbit who once turned its fur inside out for fear of moths.

—*Minou Drouet, extract from a notebook*

Contents

I

A job does things to a person, deducts a person pretty brutally from life. Desks are terrible places, no matter how many wheels a chair might have. You can't do much about how drawers fill up.

—Gary Lutz

OFFICE: GOOD STUFF OLD DOMINION TAXIDERMY

Do it the right way and the prowl gets put back
into the tall grasses behind the tract houses the
highway pins

to the skinny

acres, the less desirable acres. The pelt and claw
get remembered, get to resemble their former
habits of borrow and crawlspace

and slink the backyard

landfills for busted deckchairs and wigs to nest in.

This is how you might resume where you left off:
penmanship tailored to feedlot plus hitchhike.

This is how the professional mounts the folds
of a leftover body, easing the wood wool through

the form   removing the dead from its

muscle. Skulk and drove and bone dust braced in
the plaster,

          my poor

pet fox whose eyes, closeup, are so clear, so bright,
the shrubline fixed in the distance of them
          the rabbit's torn up ear   pink

petals of insulation tufting the ditch and there, see

the bramble snared
glint of the

noose

held there   hardwired to the nothing that's

left of it.

OFFICE: CPA OFFICE NEAR STEAKHOUSE AND ALL-BRANDS SEW & VAC

Here, in the advent
of the third-to-last
season of the very
long war, we grow
accustomed. Daresay
we grow monotonous
with task as the epic
war carries on just
over there. Arduously
monotonous as if
trekking an Everest
of even more
Everest proportions
while meting out sips
from the tin canteen
tucked clumsily
in our doeskin
sash. The hours
grow labored
with our posthumous
reckoning as invoice
after invoice
we measure
every proper
animal's worth:
flocked or pitiless
or howling.

OFFICE: COASTAL OFFICE OF OCEANIC AND ATMOSPHERIC RESEARCH

This morning someone called about a bag of dead goats
on the shoreline.   I'm sorry, I said, you mean Animal

Control but took down the memo

anyway in shorthand.

Those drowned animals deserved, at the very least, a notation:

A notation, at least, to shepherd them:

From the military duffle in olive drab straight from the factory

then padlocked then hoisted.

Hoisted waterlogged left half a mile from the highway,

the canvas in patches rent by hooves,

rent in patches by teeth the canvas.

I spent the rest of the day at my post in the

Tragedy Room, typing reports of

tornado devastation to a file called Extreme Weather

Events of the 1900s.

I copied captions to photographs, like *All that was left of the*

Newport family's home, a washing machine next to an empty foundation

and *Carried by the storm a quarter mile, five horses hitched to the same rail were the only survivors.*

OFFICE: WAREHOUSE OF THE CUT-RATE
MANUFACTURER OF SMALL LEATHER GOODS

Little flags of littered cups scatter the weed-studded lot, delete

      the rush from half wind. Inside, we hook and needle to stall,
unseam the gauges of our pockets, spray off our industrial boots

      as the belts get loaded down with the middle split. The manager

hedges his bets. Why won't Sweden export their hides? I don't know.
      They want to keep their Stockholm. What do you call a cow

with no legs? A jacket, he says, then taps the conveyor. Or ground beef. What's the dif

anyway, there's nowhere to go to get away from the machine
      of it: even up in the breakroom stinks from milk of lime,

      which is where the day stalls, post-lunch, pre-truck

and we retie our jumpsuit necks, stick our nicotine gum
      under the table. Not much goes on. Bored forklift drivers

drill shorthand graffiti on throwaway buckskin. The rest

      of us just kind of stand around, pounding each other
          in the shoulder, like surprise. Sorry for ourselves,

sorry in spite of ourselves, sorry for what we have taken.

OFFICE: DEPARTMENT OF THE LOST AND FOUND

Whatever have you come here for, the basement
        of a building near the turnpike.

Discards and burglaries pile
        up by early afternoon, like always,

lord over this office of our winter's machine: the wreckage
        of the ship still wedged hull-deep

in the permanent glacier. The wreckage of the ship,
        a bear suit, penknife and hunting knife and so on.

Statuette of a lion given over, who knows, put it with
        the statuette of the penguin.

Poor drop-in with your grief-heavy
        voice, take back your map of polar drift;

take back your mechanical leg.
        Poor, dear drop-in with your grief-heavy

mouth, take back your McMurdo Station, and
        the solitary southernmost ATM,

and the ice-breaker crushing the harbor, day in and day out,
        this muscular opera of finders keepers.

Take back your overcast biding;

                take back your weatherproof throat.

OFFICE: STATION OF THE HARNESSMAKER

Rode my bike to the ditches & ditched

it on the whip

                of plot unbound & barren

somewhat alone some-

what broken   was a horse

I lassoed him home,

               hoof & ragged

What I mean by pony-

up

               I built a supply chain of dedicated

furrows.

He roams   & I plan the perfect evening,

Twin Peaks on tape rigged up in the carport.

Agent Dale Cooper

                    is a good name for a horse,

I thought,

                    & called him in from the pallets of stride

I will not hitch,

                    muscle I will not blinder.

OFFICE: IN THE FINANCIAL SERVICES HEADQUARTERS

Dragged from the chandelier
graveyard and kept polished

in the lobby. All the managers
shuffle through,

taking out their ledgers.
Acronym after acronym

the world contracts,
mimeographs get passed

around, someone starts the
numbers. A shorthand:

manila-colored skirts and
cold knees.

Thin khakis rising briefly
at the ankles.

We finish our reports
and answer our phones,

tucked behind particle board
dividers. We unwrap our

sandwiches. While
twenty miles east of here

the blue-muzzled doe skirts
the fairgrounds to nose

orange peels and hubcaps,
skittering off on clothespin legs

at the sound of a truck short-
cutting home. No windows so

we compromise. So we hang
calendars with thumbtacks.

Wild Hoofbeats: America's
Wild Horses or *Western*

Wilderness. We make modern
American field notes to after

hours and the white noise
machine:

turn it up. Turn it up
so loud the fake silence

avalanches the mountain
of copier paper, avalanches

emergency faxes over
the supply room desk,

avalanches memos over
the terrible carpet

that hides the concrete
hallways that connect

all the breakrooms
to all the restrooms
to all the conference rooms

named after native
woodland creatures.

OFFICE: BUILDING THE LIBRARY OF WATER, STYKKISHÓLMUR, ICELAND

& morning after morning for three weeks straight

we hauled plastic coolers up through the fog

> up to the edge-of-town promontory, to the backdoor

of the former library corrugated

> into the wind & the weather

> reports us kneeling, again, this morning,

up early tucking cloth into the bottom

> of the buckets to archive

& commissary

the rubber mats we trundle, unstack, the rubber tubing we rig to derive glacier

> from glacier siphoned into rubber jugs, the waters named St. Joseph's

> Baby Aspirin, named Bootleg,

> named Broken Settlement Letter,

> named Lighthouse,

we catalogued them

according to our limited apprehension of the parts of native things,

tourists but not tourists

                                    & therefore not lugging anything

back home. Not returning but romantically to the source, see:

jokull slaked westward across oil

cloth in the back of the flatbed

we drive uphill, where we will arrange this new Testimony of Pitch & Flood,

this coastal tableau we devised, this horse

the color of milk.

OFFICE: FAILING CONSUMER ELECTRONICS CORPORATION

Made a real go of it but got kind of dumber
despite trying hard not to get dumber.
Seasons came & seasons went
while I heated up my lunches.
A blow-up parrot holding a blow-up
Corona just swinging from the rafters.
breakroom posters regarding lawsuits
regarding workers comp
regarding sexual harassment:
cartoon arm in a cartoon sling
plus a CONFIDENTIAL clip-art briefcase.
We sold car stereos, HD TVs & coaxial
cables. We sold dog toys
& sleeping bags & bouncy
kingdoms. Metallica said Boredom sets
into the boring mind. Of course
I thought about where I'd gone wrong
& pretended not to recognize the guy
from high school when I passed him
in the hallway.
I thought a lot about defeat
& then I knew what I was paid for.
Tolstoy said Boredom is the desire
for desires. How utterly &
altogether I desired for desires
slouched at my desk, unable to practice

a better posture
in the contrived emergency of
the neither here nor there
beige corridor after beige corridor
& miles of sprawled out office park: acres
of asphalt and a manmade lake
impersonating an oasis.
Impersonating an oasis so close
to the road sometimes geese
got smashed by impatient commuters.
Cleanup man with a garbage bag,
plastic billowed in the reach.
Poor birds. Poor man who had to surrender them.
I petitioned HR for a GEESE CROSSING sign.
Someone from the county called
it against code, something about
Minimum Warrant & Minimum Criteria.
Are you very embarrassed?
To tell you the truth
the job was bearable enough to keep
on with for longer than I care
to admit, daily or mostly
I guess.
What I mean is:
the sad animal & the sad man & the sad desk
carry on but: enough already.

OFFICE: SOUTHSIDE UNEMPLOYMENT COMMISSION

And after the half-hearted leave-takings.

And after the legalese, the broad signature thrust
and bestowed upon, to compose an ending.
That clutch of papers.
Thickset wrists visible beneath the ex-boss's professional sleeves.

And after my position was eliminated:
the dismantling and the putting forth in boxes.

After the search and subsequent escort:
thus, annulled.

And after.

And elsewhere, in the ruined afternoon of impermanence and daytime TV
in the flickering light of which I cut my hair
off with the kitchen scissors.

And after, for months, the radio reports.
And towns boarded up, and empty coal cars bedding the outskirt tracks,
and clearance sales, and trembling woods gaunt with trembling deer.

We were on the brink of a strange harvest.

We were waiting it out in a city graved by the smallest vaccines,
rendered to symptom and rust and murmur and all through the winter
feral dogs scammed the corner for bread crusts and chicken bones.

And we watched them hollow out.

THEY ARE TAKING THE ANIMALS OUT OF THE OFFICES

one by one.

Taking away their badges.

Wiping their heart rates clean

from the monitors & cutting

all the wires.

& the animals fidget, trying out their legs

& the animals inhale exhale

testing out their rabbit lungs,

gather up their riot & tender & resign

the sick light

of their desk lamps,

tearing up their blotters.

They are done with this pitch

& toil;

done with this industry,

fluorescent in the trenches—

the burrow & stink of it

the long & the short of it

the supply & demand of it

the patent applied for & pending of it

the blood & the bile & the skin & the milk of it

The animals are leaving

the offices one by

one

       & they run
       & they run
       & they run
       & they run
       & they

II

Animals I never saw

I with no voice

remembering names to invent for them

—*W.S. Merwin*

THE TRUE BOOK OF ANIMAL HOMES

And in the dark patches they root

a shape to settle   they flatten

the grass,
               nettle & flashweed

sometimes

to nibble on   shot up &

tumbled at the brink of a ditch,

a treeline.

& in the dark they root their way to sleep

   flattening in the quick of it

          the night just going on going on

::

::

If they are alone they huddle for warmth

scrub denned, lichen snouted

If they are not alone they huddle for warmth

furred & furrowed,

        trundle of heartbeats muzzled

        in the leaf pile

::

::

Some of them are hide-in-plain-sights
Some of them are stays-in-cages
Some of them are fleet in passage
Some are sprung and roam the grounds

::

Some are flat raced twelve

furlongs on turf tracks,

their muscles perfect

fractions of slow

twitch fast twitch, spurs

hooking rib swale pressed

toward the purse that flask

shaped man will cash

for a yacht when the horse

stops running

her slow trot warmdown

on remodeled

bones.

::

::

Some are ridden on trails tamped   through the outfield

of Prescott, Arizona, all the way

to pasture in the growing taller & taller weeds

until their coats   thin to chaff.

Threshing wind.

::

::

Some are innumerable

Some are stacked in cages in a shed
on the west side of Baltimore or

a dark barn in Lancaster, PA
on a grip of flaxen hayfield

& here comes the Amish boy
    who flings Alpo mashed with chicken
    feed through the mesh wire
    dark

& the *blackness goes leaking out*

& all the small questions getting softer

Some scurry for years

Some are sold by the road like jam like chairs like bonnets

What's invisible

the cages or the sheds or the barns,
how their callused bellies drag

whelp-heavy & freckled

::

::

Some are prizes

Some are hunted & crumpled

one by one in the marsh
in the backcountry
in the Flint Hills tallgrass prairie
their skin thrown down
on the table & zipped up
into the shape of the myth
of the victory to
hang on a wall
hang in a room

      : an arrangement
convincing
enough :

      the best representation
      of the best representation

of an elk
of an owl
of a wolf

::

Some of them are embalmed ones

Some of them are *time that does
not measure itself*

Some are drawn with a very fine camelhair brush

::

::

Some are chained to backyard treadmills

Some have strayed so far from the coast

Some rush headlong & they scramble

Some are part pit bulls part Rottweil butchers' dogs

Some pace outside the Laser
Quest on Saturday & follow
anyone home through the dead
afternoon, same as all the others
pitching across the city's back
roads & riverbanks
& drug-free school zones
& woods
& alleys
& northbound tracks
& the whole trafficked expanse of it :

                if they keep running forever

                if they are pulled restless by forage little

                by little turning back

                into wolves

::

::

Some are muscular with the fastest joy

Some are lost

Some are feasting on mulberries behind the heat pump

Some are those who are too many
        whose ancient hearts are measured against their
                turning-white fur

& every seven days the woman
    whose job it is draws
    each from his kennel
    to the end of the hall
    to the cold steel table
& touches his nose his
    head the twitching flags
    of his ears & pinches
    the syringe into his
    shoulder
& waits
& waits
& strokes his soft soft fur
    until he falls away, into

What does or doesn't come next

                    : infinite meadow of remarkable smells
                    & grazing the tall fescue in the sun
                    & black bees sleeping in the red clover
                    & the sunlight deep then deeper the
                    crepe myrtle in bloom & somewhere
                    the door to a house opens

::

Some are ones given less time

Some are ones that humans fail

Some are a *procession of clouds*

Some root for crickets & moths, sharp little
beaks scraping dirt from dirt

::

& some with a field to stand in

::

Some are those slumped & tethered out back of the market

that's a front for some other kind of market

at the corner of 24th & M.

Some are those sprawled in the dead grass on the hottest weekend

of the heat advisory summer,

no bucket of water to cool their parched

& panting no slip of shade

The one between the garbage &

the fence charges hard at whatever

rattles the chain link

& the man who runs the corner

keeps watch from upstairs

backdoor propped open with a brick.

::

Some are those that belong to the Emperor

Some are those that are trained

Some are those that, from a long way off, look like flies

::

Here they come, sifted from the dark woods, prowling & shifty.

Here they come, the mongrel ghosts of my heart.

Here they come, in folds coaxed &.

Here they come, halting—half-wild, rawboned, keen—

::

::

Some graze on lupine that clutch

the glaciers

& wander acres of dust

& cotton grass,   the wind

a grip a bluster at the scruff of their necks

as they sniff & keep nosing through crowberry :

Those who tiptoe the rocks

               & tromp the sedges

who snack on clover in the bright

of March

Little fleece machines, little woolmakers

who clutter through the fog,
who gallop across the lava fields

Those who must come in from the field now,

               those who must return to the fold now,

those who must be shorn :

::

::

Some are those branded with the *wound of steadfast longing toward*

Some are suckling pigs

Some are gathered, hauled & penned

stampede of pink snouts stampede of dirty feathers

docked & unloaded & crammed

into dead space: such various prying &

no inch to scamper

        & nothing good remains intact :
        beak
        or tail
        or plumage
        or hoof.

::

Some are those that pace in terror

Some are those that cower in shame

Some are those that tremble as if they were mad

Some are those included in this classification

::

Some are those that look like they've just broken a flower vase.

Some are those who rove & stomp

                              hoof by hoof

a lapsing trot,   a lumbering

those big moony eyes

filling up the whole pasture,

                              they take you in.

::

Some rabbit in the gulches

                  & burrow by firstlight

or roost in the shallows

roost in the needle-&-thread

of their apple bed warbling,

warbling.

Oh littles

      full of scaffold &

      clover

They come to find us

           : they come to body us home

III

We are all jittery animals who doubt ourselves.

—Dear Polly advice column

ESSAY ON URBAN HOMESTEADING

The dumb hours blunt the after
        noon with bottleneck

with clover & weeds
        almost meadowed

& black widows & the mint.
        There are so many ways

to be tired. All summer list
        & ungather, place strategic

plywood over yielding
        planks. The beginning

a swelter now settled :
        now not new :

We have our pick of bars
        & a new bullet

ratio : a little less day-to-day
        interruption : a little less

metal : barrel : slate : syringe.
        Less watch-how-the-dark

-performs-our-ghosts.
        We settle in,

accommodate the history
       of what is left

to us, blue marl & viaduct,
       cold storage units

turned into lofts; sirens
       & blackouts;

a rampage of ten-year-old boys
       throwing rocks.

ESSAY ON ECONOMIES OF SCALE

Mid-morning they arrive.

I'm at the grocery fingering

cellophane tucked slick

to the iceberg lettuce.

As the summer school kids

trade cigarettes & sleeping

pills down at the pipeline.

It's mid-morning & late afternoon & another day.

First tomatoes ripening

by the fistful.

It's early July when they arrive

dusty arrive heat stroked

arrive like so many boxes

of catalytic converters

& the day splits open,   squeal

& prodded.

Day dragged forth.

When the phone rings & it's no one.

While I'm waiting for an oil change at the service station.

As daylight wanes & fireflies lamp

the backyard as the heatwave stretches

into a third week & the city's power

goes out/goes on/flickers again

when the storm comes.

They arrive grimed to cages & truck stuffed to capacity:

delivery distribution problem solved.

Thursday morning & any morning

& daily & weekly

& half-past ten.

This morning on the kill floor

the piglet tried to nuzzle the worker   Like a puppy,

the worker says, It happens all the time.

& by then the international flight is canceled

& by then the library books are overdue

& by then the new pop songs have replaced the new pop songs

& by then like two ships passing

& by then the petition has been circulated

& by then the signatures pending

& by then we are all dolled up

& by then we have gone dancing

& by then the raffle's ended & a man has won the Sebring

& by then the GDP

& by then the private-sector benefits

& by then per capita

& by then the joke doesn't land

& by then dinner's ready

& by then the season coming on

& by then the committees gathering

& the committees all forming ghost committees

& the TV shows starting up again

ESSAY ON THE NEW YEAR

In the byzantine days
of the newest year
there were no good
answers. I showed up
at parties with the same
old lament; indeed I was
slow to cultivate
decorum. Slow to give
up the ghost of the heart
that has been meager.
A heart like the ruined
cloakroom of November
with its Sears hunting
plaid, cashier's check
still in the pocket.
To give up the ghost:
to relinquish this ailment,
how it tempers.
All around me histories
converged. The hours
of footnote and tremble.
The sack that slackens
at the bottom of the
river, snug with a litter
of kittens. Who's to say
how we go on or don't
go on, despairing
unspecifically.
That thy misery be
known for what it is:
vernacular, of
an interior sea.

ESSAY ON ALBUQUERQUE

Gallows' birches ghost up
the timberland, pitched sleek.
Hardly any limbs and shiftless
save for anemic gusts of wind
that do not remove anything
but dust. If dust. Neither here
nor there we scavenger,
we pickpocket, like it's our day job,
this tomorrowing.
Over gourd stems and bottle
caps we traipse and collect,
our spoony shadows elking
the midday. This trial and error
of the westward ho. What to claim
or not, how to guess what any
leave-taking will require
the farther you get from familiar.
Out of gloom, and coveting, miles
of quarantine and pilgrimage.
Approaching a fable.
Then fabled.

ESSAY ON THE HOMEOPATHIC TREATMENT FOR HUMAN LONGING

There was no more time already.
It had all run out.
What was there to do about it
besides sit here, on this bench
behind the rented farmhouse
and memorize the winter light
holding the leaves down cold.
I didn't do much else.
I fed the goats raisins.
I finished my cup of coffee.
I thought of the unbearable news
of the day before which followed
the unbearable news of the day
before that and I stared at the
useless trees.

Late in the afternoon the deer came,
haltingly, through the dusk
of the woods to press
in a cluster this field. I counted
seven. Soft darknesses
threading into
darker shadows.
Going somewhere, on the way
to somewhere, already disappearing.

ESSAY ON AN INDEPENDENT ASSESSMENT of the TECHNICAL FEASIBILITY of the MARS ONE MISSION PLAN

Introduction

The idea is

human settlement

on the surface

of

a departure

approximately

All systems are

atmospheric

and   drawn

from

the Mean Time Between Failures,

which means:

there's a little time;   but

how far into time

      can *later* come

      or be carried?

A brief background

    A brief summary of the

    solar arrangements

    & an oven

    to extract water from

        the northern

    latitude,

    the wet areas

    of redundancy—

A Plan

The crew departs earth,

makes   an open-loop:

the cycle of sending

continues every

26 months,

          allowing the

settlement to   expand

over time.

Analysis focus

We apply our Mars

What we are building

we are building upon

a scaled-up version

of a handful of plant experiments

//

Listen: space

systems compose

  the entire performance

          of input values

&

Life Support Technologies

smoothen this

          horizon—

Spanning time

between a common repeating

;   for instance,

A constellation program:

a dedicated chamber

of impacts inside impacts.

//

What Mars might look like:

densely packed shelves of light.

//

—

imagine—

being the first

to reach the farthest

reaches.

Results and discussion

Note:

Changes In The Mass Of

Changes To The Loads On

Changes In The Number Of

Changes In The Probability

For   Each

    Spare

    Life.

Conclusion

After these mission days,

to determine horizon

is to determine

deficiencies.

We just come up against

the facts:

            an exponential equation

is calculated and so we assume

a given

a threshold

we assume an entire assembly of light

ESSAY ON THE BODY

Are you animal, then—

are you gallop   scape

of   fringecup & wood-sorrel & sweet

after death   are you rove the pines   are you plush

the thicket—

Body goes in a flash   in a fever in a rush, scrapping

Body goes all this time

Goes hooked to the ache   & seasons   standing in the pits,

junk carnival long   gone just the outskirts then the outskirts

around that   What kingdom of death is this? To heave in the dust

of the outfield, the loose split,

we surplus   & hostage the meat of your plenty.

No-name electric, harness & shackle.

All those summers   Body left to un

creature.   The dig & gnaw of waiting

was a plague.

Nobody came, nobody came.

ESSAY ON VIBRANT MATTER

The first, best, perfect
remedy,   a slake

a salve
a wound

of spent
stars

for the suture.

The wreckage collects
inside,

rabbiting the rabbit

in all of us little

by little
adding up

to something
feral.

Tonight at the bar
the chalkboard over

our heads says
bone marrow cake

is the dessert
of the day

and I get it: the point
is to devour

to oblivion
our fetish

isn't it
wild, this disease, how it glows

almost nuclear
at the source,

how we take every chance
we get

to glow brighter
than the brightest thing

we can get our hands
on

the first chance
we get

every chance
we get

closer to
how it glows

almost nuclear
at the source—

If there was a way, at least,

to see by the light

of it

spilling out

OH LITTLE FOX

Could wildly;

        could wilder.

Little radar in the burrow

        and the underbrush   and the

empty rabbit tunnel. Little

        concierge in the blackberries,

in the new south,

        behind the field

house,

        in the brambles.   Little ache

in the inventory,

        folding the forest

in half.

NOTES

ESSAY ON THE ECONOMIES OF SCALE is after and indebted to Idra Novey's poem, "Meanwhile the Watermelon Seed"

ESSAY ON THE HOMEOPATHIC TREATMENT FOR HUMAN LONGING takes its title from the artist Dario Robleto's work called "A Homeopathic Treatment for Human Longing": *Glass vials, vintage glass electrode wands, 19th-century bloodletting cupping glass, various artist-made homeopathic remedies (sound of glaciers melting, voice of oldest to ever live, last heartbeats of loved one, million-year-old blossom, million-year-old raindrop, deceased lovers' heartbeats, extinct animal sounds, extinct languages), various custom-ordered remedies made by professional homeopath (black amber, willow, tears, mammoth hair, glacial runoff, voice of oldest widow, black swan bone dust, Silvia Plath's voice), velvet, silk, leather, ribbon, brass, iron, cork, pine, typeset, 66 x 129 x 53 ¼ inches. 2008.*

THE LIBRARY OF WATER is artist Roni Horn's long-term installation housed in a former library in the small coastal town of Stykkishólmur, Iceland. The library is a 24-volume collection of floor-to-ceiling water cylinders, each containing water from one of the 24 glaciers of Iceland—including the now extinct Ok glacier.

OFFICE: BUILDING THE LIBRARY OF WATER is for Barbara Yien, who brought the glimmering repository to my attention.

ESSAY ON URBAN HOMESTEADING is for Joshua Poteat and Church Hill.

ESSAY ON THE HOMEOPATHIC TREATMENT FOR HUMAN

LONGING is for, and in memory to, Jake Adam York.

THE TRUE BOOK OF ANIMAL HOMES uses parts of Jorge Borges' "Celestial Emporium of Benevolent Knowledge's Taxonomy" as a framework throughout.

p. 24: *blackness goes leaking out* is Anne Carson's
p. 25: "the best representation/of the best representation" is taken from Dave Madden's *The Authentic Animal: Inside the Odd and Obsessive World of Taxidermy*
p. 25: "time that does not measure itself" is taken from Clarice Lispector's *Agua Viva*
p. 28: "procession of clouds" borrows phrasing from Aracelis Girmay's poem, "Small Letter"
p. 32: "wound of steadfast longing" comes from Julian of Norwich's *Revelations of Divine Love*

THE TRUE BOOK OF ANIMAL HOMES is dedicated to Ruben, Piper, Elly, and Daisy.

ESSAY ON AN INDEPENDENT ASSESSMENT of the TECHNICAL FEASIBILITY of the MARS ONE MISSION PLAN is an erasure of a 35-page feasibility report prepared by scientists at MIT.

VIBRANT MATTER was originally written for MA Keller's Abaculi Project.

For the book's epigraph, I am indebted to AM Marshall.

Allison Titus is the author of *Sum of Every Lost Ship* and *The Arsonist's Song Has Nothing to Do With Fire.*

Winners of the Saturnalia Books Poetry Prize:

Telepathologies by Cortney Lamar Charleston

Ritual & Bit by Robert Ostrom

Neighbors by Jay Nebel

Thieves in the Afterlife by Kendra DeColo

Lullaby (with Exit Sign) by Hadara Bar-Nadav

My Scarlet Ways by Tanya Larkin

The Little Office of the Immaculate Conception by
Martha Silano

Personification by Margaret Ronda

To the Bone by Sebastian Agudelo

Famous Last Words by Catherine Pierce

Dummy Fire by Sarah Vap

Correspondence by Kathleen Graber

The Babies by Sabrina Orah Mark

Also Available from saturnalia books:

Sweet Insurgent by Elyse Fenton

Plucking the Stinger by Stephanie Rogers

The Tornado Is the World by Catherine Pierce

Steal It Back by Sandra Simonds

In Memory of Brilliance and Value by Michael Robins

Industry of Brief Distraction by Laurie Saurborn Young

That Our Eyes Be Rigged by Kristi Maxwell

Don't Go Back to Sleep by Timothy Liu

Reckless Lovely by Martha Silano

A spell of songs by Peter Jay Shippy

Each Chartered Street by Sebastian Agudelo

No Object by Natalie Shapero

Nowhere Fast by William Kulik

Arco Iris by Sarah Vap

The Girls of Peculiar by Catherine Pierce

Xing by Debora Kuan

Other Romes by Derek Mong

Faulkner's Rosary by Sarah Vap

Tsim Tsum by Sabrina Orah Mark

Hush Sessions by Kristi Maxwell

Days of Unwilling by Cal Bedient

Gurlesque: the new grrly, grotesque, burlesque poetics
edited by Lara Glenum and Arielle Greenberg

*Letters to Poets: Conversations about Poetics, Politics,
and Community*
edited by Jennifer Firestone and Dana Teen Lomax

Artist/Poet Collaboration Series:

Velleity's Shade by Star Black / Artwork by Bill Knott

Polytheogamy by Timothy Liu / Artwork by Greg Drasler

Midnights by Jane Miller / Artwork by Beverly Pepper

Stigmata Errata Etcetera by Bill Knott /
Artwork by Star Black

Ing Grish by John Yau / Artwork by Thomas Nozkowski

Blackboards by Tomaz Salamun /
Artwork by Metka Krasovec

The True Book of Animal Homes was printed using
the fonts Avant Garde and Adobe Garamond